Joyce Rupp

PRAYERS

TO

SOPHIA

*Deepening Our Relationship
with Holy Wisdom*

AUTHOR OF *OPEN THE DOOR*

SORIN BOOKS   Notre Dame, IN

© 2000, 2004, 2010 Joyce Rupp

www.sorinbooks.com

ISBN-10 1-893732-84-3   ISBN-13 978-1-893732-84-1

Cover image © istockphoto.

Cover and text design by Katherine Robinson Coleman.

Printed and bound in the United States of America.

Library of Congress Cataloging-in-Publication Data is available from the Library of Congress.

To Elizabeth Schmidt,
passionate child,
who awakened me to
Sophia's presence in my life

To Ruth Butler,
wise woman,
who walked with me on
my first journey with Sophia

CONTENTS

ACKNOWLEDGMENTS

I n the ten years since I first wrote about Sophia in *The Star in My Heart,* there have been many who have blessed me with their affirmation and encouragement. I am deeply grateful to all who have participated in my conferences and retreats and who have shared their experience of Sophia with me. I am equally grateful to those who have taken the time to write, telling me how much *The Star in My Heart* drew them into a new or deeper relationship with Sophia.

When I completed the first draft of these prayers, I sent them to selected individuals and asked for a critique. What wonderful help each of these readers gave. Their wisdom and insights were a great gift to me as I honed and shaped the prayers and journaling suggestions. I offer my heartfelt thanks to: Frank and Ruth Butler, Judith Cauley, Patricia deJong, Kathleen O'Daniel, and Margaret Ann Schmidt.

One of the joys of creating these prayers was being able to work with Innisfree publisher Marcia Broucek. Her wise expertise and her collaborative approach have been such a blessing. She has been a literary midwife for me as we worked together to bring *Prayers to Sophia* to birth.

There are numerous others whom I want to thank, but I will name just a few: my mother, Hilda, whose innate wisdom continues to inspire my life; the many who promise to pray for me each day, especially Janet Barnes and Dorothy Sullivan; my good friend Macrina Wiederkehr, whose encouragement and creativity cause my own to come to birth; and my Service community, in particular, Eleanor Gait, who has done so much to support and market my work.

Most of all, I thank Sophia, the Wise and Radiant One, who amazes me with the journey on which she leads me and the guidance that she constantly provides. All of the prayers in this book have her mark of grace and goodness as a foundation. None would have come to life without her daily, abiding presence.

INTRODUCTION

It has been ten years since I wrote *The Star in My Heart: Discovering Inner Wisdom.* When I think about how that book came to birth, I am still amazed. In the preface to *The Star in My Heart,* I explained how I had no intention of writing about Divine Wisdom until the moment when I saw my friend's two-year-old daughter, Elizabeth, dancing around, smelling the flowers in her family's rose garden. Even then I did not comprehend that what had surfaced in my consciousness was a connection with the beautiful verse from Proverbs 8 in which Sophia describes herself as playing in the universe at the time of creation. As I contemplated the young, dancing child in the rose garden, I found myself taking pen and paper and beginning to write about Holy Wisdom. That moment gave rise to *The Star in My Heart.*

Elizabeth is now a budding young woman. She has grown a lot. So have I. At the time when Elizabeth danced among the flowers in a Sophia-like posture, I barely knew that "Sophia" was the Greek word for Wisdom. I did know how unusual it is to have Wisdom referred to as "she" and "her" in the Bible and that it is rare to have any biblical references about the feminine as a divine quality. However, I had only a tiny awareness of the depth and the beauty found in the scriptural passages referring to Sophia. I had been attracted to wisdom for a long time, but my cultural conditioning had kept me viewing wisdom as a "thing," as a quality or a characteristic of the Divine but not the Divine herself. The Biblical wisdom texts do contain wise sayings (things), such as those in Proverbs, but they also contain passages that refer directly to wisdom as a person.

It was only when I prayerfully dwelt inside the scripture passages that contain the "wisdom literature," that I really came to a personal relationship with Sophia. I moved from viewing "wisdom" as a quality of the Divine One to perceiving "Wisdom" as the Divine One herself. It was then that I began naming Sophia as the One for whom I have yearned and the One whom I have known for a long, long time. Since then, after nearly ten years of praying daily to the Divine in the name of Sophia, I realize in a much fuller way how deeply and tenderly she is a part of me.

Having said this, I also want to note that I believe all our names for the Divine, whether male or female, are inadequate. All these metaphors are our feeble human attempts and projections as we try to draw near to the Mysterious One. Probably the only adequate name for the Holy One is that which was written long ago: "I Am Who I Am" (Exodus 3:14). In order to have a personal relationship, however, it is helpful to name the Divine. "Sophia" has become the

best divine name for my prayer. I resonate immensely with her qualities of guidance, truth-bringing, and
companionship. She is always with me as I search for
the way home, which is what I am consistently doing
on my spiritual path.

How Others Respond to Sophia

I remember how scared I was when a colleague
of mine, a very critical thinker, read a part of the
manuscript for *The Star in My Heart*. When she
returned the pages to me, she challenged me with:
"So, is Sophia divine?" I remember feeling alarm and
concern. Would I be rejected or considered heretical
if I said what I thought: "Yes, of course, she is one of
the unique manifestations of the divine." Instead, I
replied, "I'm not sure." Years later I smile at my early
fears because now I know what a comfort and a joy
Sophia is to me, and I never think of her as being
anything other than the true Source of Life. I have
also stopped being concerned about what others will
think of me because I pray to Sophia.

In my travels and in my ministry, I have come to
know that there is a great deal of anger and fear within the Christian community regarding Sophia. Many
Christians brush her off with the dismissal of "It's a
New Age thing." It pains me every time I hear that
comment because I realize how much spiritual richness they are missing. I also wonder if they have ever
reflected on the wisdom texts in the Bible. The deeper

issue is, I believe, that Sophia represents the feminine side of the Holy One. This approach to God-ness incites them to speak fearfully or angrily about heresy and condemnation. When I go back and remember my hesitations and concerns as I first began to think about Sophia as a manifestation of the Divine, I can more readily understand their hesitation and their refusal to accept Sophia.

It has been a great joy to me, though, to hear positive comments repeatedly from those who have discovered Sophia through *The Star in My Heart.* Letters have come from many places and from a variety of persons, both young and old, male and female. A number of these are older women who have written such things as, "I feel as though I have finally come home," "I have found a friend in Sophia," and "I have always longed to be able to relate to God in this way."

One of my true moments of joy was the time I was giving a conference on grief and loss. After the break, an older man stood up and he said, "Could you speak a bit about Sophia? My spiritual director introduced me to her, and it has been the best thing that has ever happened in my spiritual growth." I wanted to hug that man (and I did at the next break) for giving me an opportunity to speak about Sophia.

Sad to say, even those who find Sophia as their newly discovered divine soul-mate cannot always risk letting others know about her. I received a beautiful letter from a successful writer. She gave me permission to tell her story but not to use her name for fear that her writings would be rejected if her readers discovered that she believed in Sophia. She wrote, "There are circles in which I speak where the mention of Sophia would cause people to think my spiritual trolley had slipped off the track." Unfortunately, her fear is probably valid. I long for the day when this will change.

My Hope for This Book

My goal for *Prayers to Sophia* is to present the beauty and depth that can be found in relating to Sophia. I hope that these prayers will act as catalysts and companions for an ever deepening relationship with her. I offer these prayers as a support and enhancement of the spirituality of those who are comfortable and at ease with the Divine Feminine. I am not out to convince anyone about Sophia. I leave whatever needs to be revealed about Divine Wisdom in her hands.

All of the divine qualities named in these prayers are a reflection of the qualities attributed to the Holy One by both Jewish and Christian scriptures. A wisdom verse accompanies each of the prayers so that the "root" of the prayer can be recognized. These texts are taken from some of the wisdom literature of the Bible: Proverbs, Ecclesiasticus (Sirach), Wisdom (often called The Wisdom of Solomon), and Baruch. (The latter three are from the Apocrypha.) I hope that the scripture verses connected with each prayer will draw you to read and reflect on the wisdom passages. There is so much spiritual vitality to be gleaned from these texts of scripture.

About the Prayers

Almost all of these prayers to Sophia are from my journals. Sometimes I used just a few lines as the core of a prayer and then developed it further. Other prayers are printed almost entirely as I originally wrote them. A few are new ones that I prayed and created as I worked on the manuscript. Obviously, these prayers do not cover all the varied facets of our life experiences. I chose them somewhat at random, but when I took a closer look, I noticed that in one way or another, they all speak of Sophia's loving quality as a guide and companion. Not surprising, because I consistently look to Sophia for daily spiritual direction. My spiritual transformation depends on her graced presence in my life.

The suggestions for journaling that accompany each of the prayers are intended for your own personal exploration of your relationship with Sophia. These nudges are offered so that you can reflect on your life and discover a greater clarity about your spiritual path. May they sustain and encourage your compassionate presence in our hurting world.

Finally, I need to voice a concern about sharing these prayers with you. They may appear to be very "self-oriented." You will find "me" and "I" prevalent in these prayers. This is reflective of my relationship with Sophia. It is a very personal one. As this relationship continually unfolds, she constantly leads me deeper, challenges me to grow freer, and keeps inviting me to be more truly my best self. I know that this relationship is never just for myself. It is out of this affinity with Sophia and my ongoing transformation that I am consistently led outward to the world in which I am to give my life and service.

Sophia always draws me up and outward once I have been led down and inward. It is a cycle that I trust. I do believe that I am a much more compassionate woman for having sat in Sophia's presence. I do not know where she will lead me in the future. I only know that I am deeply grateful for having come to know and love her. It is with my heart in her heart, with joy and gratitude, that I offer the following fifty prayers to you.

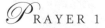

A Birthing

Holy Midwife,
you rejoiced at the birth of creation.
I hold up to you the intuited mystery
of something new being birthed in me.
It has no face, no name, no sound, no shape.
I only know that something unperceived
is meant to come to life
inside the womb of my deepest self.
Is it greater depth or valuable clarity?
Is it a whole new way of being?
I fail to understand what it might be.
My knowing is as faint as the light of a new moon.

I know I must trust in your unfailing care.
You will be attentive to this unnamed one
who struggles mightily to be released within me.
Help me to be attuned to the contractions of my spirit,
to relax when I ought and push when I must.
Encourage me to believe in what I cannot yet see.
Be by my side as I await this mysterious new life,
still curled up inside my pregnant spirit.

Let me have faith in something good slowly taking shape and be trusting enough to stay in the birthing process. Let me be willing to endure the sweat and the groans and to cheer wildly when new life comes bursting forth.

> *"When there were no depths I was brought forth, when there were no springs abounding with water . . . I was brought forth."*
> *Proverbs 8:24–25*

Journaling

Is there something in your life that is currently being birthed but still has no name?

How are you nurturing the unnamed newness?

What do you need from Sophia to midwife this birthing?

A Little Space in Which to Grow

Source of Nurturance,
I have enough space in which to grow
if I will let myself believe it.
Each moment you offer me your deep embrace.
I need only to awaken and deepen my awareness.

You can fit into the tiniest space of my life.
No place is too small for growth.
You slip into my passages of thought.
You glide through my relationships.
You flow between the creases of my work.
You pass among my many emotions.
You sail into my night dreams.
You squeeze into my busyness.
You nestle in my solitude.
Every part of my life has space enough for you.

Loving One, Source of All Growth,
I am always in that little space
where spiritual sprouting can happen,

if only I desire and welcome it.
May I be intentional about looking for you.
May I be open and aware.

> *"She will reveal her secrets to them."*
> *Ecclesiasticus 4:18*

Journaling

What are "the little spaces" of your life where you least expect to grow?

When you look inside your life, where do you especially sense Sophia's nurturance and call to greater growth?

A New Beginning

Faithful Guide,
you sit at the gate of my life,
inviting me to eagerly enter
the newness stretching before me.
As I attend to the old burdens
that have weighed me down with worry,
I look ahead with hopeful expectation
to what my heart most needs.
I also recognize the absolute necessity
of living in the present moment.
I choose to direct my daily attentiveness
toward what will give my life greater balance.
I seek to let go of what keeps me unloving.
I long to contribute to peace in this world.

Often place the mirror of truth before me
so that I can see who I am
and how I need to go about my life.
Attune me daily to the beauty in all of creation.
Embrace me with your serenity and tender mercy.
I give you my love as I walk into this new beginning.

Once again, I place my confidence in you,
faithful companion and trusted guide.
You will show me the way to wholeness.

> *"One who rises early to seek her will have no
> difficulty, for she will be found sitting at the
> gate . . ."*
> *Wisdom 6:14*

Journaling

Draw the gate of your new beginning.

Take special notice of the size, shape, and color of
this gate and its significance for you.

Ask yourself: "What do I leave behind with no
regrets? What do I hope to find as I go through this
gate?"

Draw symbols on the gate (or write words and phrases) that express your hope for the new beginning.

Anxiety

Calming Sea of Peace,
bits of anxiety rankle my spirit.
They inject distress signals
in all that I attempt to do.
My joy scurries into hiding.
Too much intensity pounds me.
Ego rah-rahs and my soul weeps.

Like the ebbing tide of the ageless sea,
I yearn to be calm, be still,
no fretting and intense beating
against the shore of myself.
But the seagulls of anxiety screech
and the wild waves press upon my life.

Wrap your care around my worries.
Allow me to absorb your peace.
Take hold of my hand, press firmly.
I need to feel your closeness
lest I fall into the pit of agitation.

I do believe in your nearness,
yet I get too caught up
in my desires, pressures, and needs.
Once again I open my being to you.
Come, Peaceful One, come!
Fill me with surrender and quiet.
Draw me into the stillness of your heart.
Together we will walk the seashore of my life.

> *"Those who listen to me will be secure and will*
> *live at ease, without dread of disaster."*
> *Proverbs 1:23*

Journaling

What kind of inner seashore do you walk on these days? Is the tide out and the beach calm? Is the tide coming in with a relentless pounding upon the shore?

What do you desire for your inner seashore as you walk with Sophia by your side?

Beauty

Irresistible Beauty,
I am often caught up in the kaleidoscope of your love
through the beautiful gifts I find in my life.
In those graced glimpses, I am swept away by gratitude
for your companionship and your constancy.
Sometimes your created beauty calls so deeply to me
that I am carried away to a place beyond,
where union with you is simple and complete.

This day it is November sunsets that draw me to you.
I gaze at the dark gray clouds hanging over
the peaceful peaks of the distant mountains,
a peach strand and a pink glow touching them.
I stay long, looking at their ever changing forms
through the barren branches of the aspen trees.

Your beauty is reflected there, everywhere.
I receive your mantle of magnificence
and wear it as a cloak around my soul.

You have brought much to me by your loveliness:
consolation, affirmation, healing, challenge, gratitude.

Thank you for your dance of divine allurement
in the secret heart of everything magnificent.
I cannot live without beauty.
I cannot live without you.

> *"She is more beautiful than the sun and excels*
> *every constellation of the stars."*
> *Wisdom 7:29*

Journaling

Where do you find beauty? How does it influence
your life?

What part of life allures you, attracts you, and draws
you nearer to Sophia?

How might Sophia bring beauty into your life?

Befriending My Aging

Companion of Life, Guardian of Death,
more and more I resemble an old gnarled tree,
wrinkled bark, gray boughs, thinning leaves.
The ground around my roots is weakening.
My limbs bend and no longer stretch very far.

Grant me the ability to not be afraid,
even in the face of significant physical change.
Be a source of deepening hope
during my internal and external adjustment.
Keep me trusting in the deepest part of myself
where love and vitality are stored.

Teach me about true and everlasting beauty,
to compassionate my body in its growing frailty,
to love my mind and heart even as my life wanes,
to befriend the wrinkles and accept the grayness,
to be unthreatened by the depletion of my energy
and the waning of a memory that was once keenly alert.

Ancient One,
fill my heart with joy in the little gifts of life.

Let me find sources of comfort and serenity
in the midst of my aches and loss.
Be near, ever-vigilant Beloved, as I experience
the creaks and groans of my aging process.
Show me how to embrace this transition time
as my soul ripens for its final journey home.

> *"When you have gray hair, you will still find
> wisdom."*
> *Ecclesiasticus 6:18*

Journaling

What do you see as the blessings of aging?

What is most difficult for you?

What kind of tree do you envision yourself to be at
this time of your life? Sketch this tree.

Calling on Sophia

Radiant and Unfading Wisdom,
your deep love calls to me.
I seek you with all my heart.
Hasten to make yourself known.

Sit at the gate of my heart.
Teach me your ways.
Meet me in my every thought.
Attune my mind to your perceptions.
Open all that is closed within me.
I desire your instruction.
I long to receive and to share your love.

Dance on the path of my life.
Free me from all that hinders.
Deepen all that attracts me to you.
As the mystery of my life unfolds
through the quickly passing years,
draw my love ever nearer to you.

I promise to be awake and vigilant,
attentive to your voice,

receptive to your guidance.
I will hide no secrets from you.
Come, reveal yourself to me.

> *"Wisdom is radiant and unfading,*
> *and she is easily discerned by those who love*
> *her, and is found by those who seek her."*
> *Wisdom 6:12*

Journaling

When do you find yourself calling upon Sophia?

For what do you most long and seek when you call upon her?

Call upon Sophia today from the depths of your heart in word or dance, song or art.

Coming Home to My Center

Steadfast Love,
enfold me with your equanimity.
Wrap me round with tender embrace.
Gather me under your sheltering wings.
Hold me in the nest of your abiding love,
for I am a scattered one today
in need of a strongly grounded center.

Vision and Guidance,
direct my every step and action
in this day that is filled with activity.
Help my truest, most loving self
to shine through all I am and all I do.
Permeate my entire being
until I sing fully of your love.

Keep me close to your heart,
where I know I belong.
Direct me to you, my Center,
where I find peace, harmony,

satisfaction, guidance,
all I need
to travel the path of life well.

Keep calling to my spirit:
"Come home! Come home!"

> *"Come to her with all your soul, and keep her
> ways with all your might."*
> *Ecclesiasticus 6:26*

Journaling

Go the center of your self. Sit with the peace that is deep within you.

When you are ready, listen to what Sophia speaks to you about coming home to your truest self.

Write this message in your journal.

Commitment

Wise and Faithful Guide,
you lovingly abide in my depths
and graciously guide my every step.
You lead me to ever stronger growth
and draw me more fully toward inner freedom.
I thank you today for the awesome ways
in which you constantly enter my life
as I pledge my heart to you again.

This day I renew my life's purpose
of being faithful to our relationship.
I give you my openness,
trusting that you will lead me on paths
that are meant to help me grow.
I re-commit my intention
to listen to you in all of life.

I promise you my daily discipleship
so that I may be an instrument of your love.
Most of all, I give you the loyalty of my heart.
May I do all in the circle of your wisdom

and learn from your dance of compassion
in every corner of this universe.

Source of Inner Luminosity,
thank you for being a loving radiance.
May the lantern of your perpetual goodness always
shine in me and through me.

> *"Do not forsake her, and she will keep you;*
> *love her, and she will guard you."*
> *Proverbs 4:6*

Reflect on what you most want to dedicate to
Sophia. Are there qualities you feel called to develop and deepen? Is there a promise that awaits your
keeping?

Write your commitment to Sophia.

Compassion

Eternal Heart of the Universe,
I am wrapped in the womb of morning.
I am one with the cooing of doves
and the green of the river's edge.
I am a part of the slowly moving water
and the grayness of the wide sky.
All of who I am turns around and walks
toward the center of my being.
I feel a oneness with all of life.

In this moment I know for certain
that each creature, insect, stone, and plant,
each woman, man, and child, young and old,
are all my sisters and my brothers.
No part of life is separate from me.
Their joy and happiness is my joy and happiness.
Their suffering and sorrow is my suffering and sorrow.

Each of us dwells within you, Womb of Love.
You are the container of our lives.
You are the source of all nourishment,

the safe hold for each of us in our vulnerability.

Eternal Heart of the Universe,
I stretch out to touch you in the myriad creations
that have danced to life from you, the Source.
Thank you for all these relatives of mine.
They will receive good care from me.

> *"Who more than she is fashioner of what*
> *exists?"*
> *Wisdom 8:6*

Journaling

Choose a "relative" in the universe who needs your attention and care (a devastated rainforest, an endangered whale, an aboriginal child, a polluted river, a political prisoner . . .)

Write a letter of love to this relative of yours.

Dance of the Universe

Passionate Presence,
dance your vibrant life within me.
Leap and bound joyfully through me.
I yearn to be centered and alive
so I can join the dance of the universe.
Help me to enter into greater oneness
with each and every part of creation.

Fill me with your enlivening vision
until I fully know that I am a sister
with all that roams, and wings, and swims.
Let your dance come bounding in me
so the trees' green springs in me,
songbirds singing becomes my singing,
the hum of the stars echoes as my hum,
lapping lake waters wash the shore in me,
and flowers' blooming tickles my soul.

Dance, Sophia, dance!
Urge my single heartbeat to join

with the ancient and ongoing heartbeat
of all that takes shape in this universe.
I long to dance your dance.

> *"Because of her pureness, she pervades and*
> *penetrates all things."*
> *Wisdom 7:22-23*

Journaling

When do you feel most "one" with all that is?

Imagine yourself to be a plant, animal, rock, or some other aspect of the universe. Enter into its existence. Dance as if you were this piece of the universe.

Write a prayer to Sophia as if it is from the "voice" of this plant, animal, rock . . .

Desire for Spiritual Growth

Gift of Mercy and Understanding,
all my good intentions
for spiritual growth
go sliding down the gutter
of responsibilities.
All my hopes
of deepening prayer
get splintered and broken
in the chaos of busyness.
All my desires
to have a quiet haven
are swallowed
in the jaws of my calendar.
All my resolutions
to rise earlier, to pray longer
are lost in the blankets
of an extra hour of sleep.

And all the while
I fuss and fume about this,
you look at me and smile.
Are you sending me the message
that spiritual growth can happen
among the very things
that seem to keep me from you?
Are you assuring me
that my desire to grow
is not lost to you?

> *"Wisdom cries out in the street; . . . at the busiest corner she cries out."*
> *Proverbs 1:20–21*

Journaling

What in your life calls you to spiritual growth?

What seems to keep you from spiritual growth?

What growth is taking place in you at this time?

What assurance do you need from Sophia?

Draw Me
to Your Heart

Wise and Faithful Guide,
keep my spirit entwined with yours.
Teach me about the poor and the pained.
Fill me with your mercy and compassion.
Help me to find your peace in my troubled moments.
Let love be the response I give to those who oppose me.
Constantly draw me toward all that is good.

Urge me to give my best to those who need it.
Lead me to learn from my discouragement and struggles.
Be the light I need to find my way in the darkness.
Fill my hollowness and emptiness with your love.

Most of all, continue to dwell within me
because your gracious presence is all I ever need.
It is enough to bring me through the deepest canyons
and the darkest crevices of my life.

Divine Companion,
draw me to your heart where wisdom resides
and daily let me choose to follow in your way.

> *"I loved her more than health or beauty, and I*
> *chose to have her rather than light, because*
> *her radiance never ceases."*
> *Wisdom 7:10*

Journaling

What is it that you seek from this Wise and Faithful
Guide?

Draw a heart and place some words or symbols on
it to represent what you seek.

Evening

Mother of the Weary,
grant me your evening blessing.
Rock my spirit into peacefulness.
Ease my cares away from me.
Nest in the home of my heart
and cradle my life in your love.

As I gaze back upon the day
that I have just traveled with you,
accept my gratitude for the joys
and my sorrow for the failings.
Abiding Peace, bestow upon me,
and upon all who dwell on earth:
your protective shelter in our sleep,
your guarding presence from all harm,
your perceptive spirit in our dreams.

First Star of the Evening,
be the strong light in my heart.
Shine brightly while I slumber.
Abide with me in tender vigilance

so that I will arise in the morning
with my soul awakened in your love.

> *". . . all her paths are peace."*
> *Proverbs 3:17*

Journaling

Sit with dusk. Let the calm of evening descend upon
you. Rest with Sophia.

Look back over your day.

How and what did Sophia teach you?

Failings and Mistakes

Heart of Mercy,
my mistakes and failings keep me humble.
They chide me with their blaming voices
and pester me with their mocking comments.
They badger me with their poking fingers
of disgrace and condemnation.
They hound me with blame and guilt
and a thousand other recriminations.

Walk with me through my mistakes and failings.
Let me hear your understanding and merciful voice.
We both know that I am not a perfect person.
Assure me that I am not a bad person, either.
Keep teaching me about myself, about life, about you,
through these characteristics
I would much rather not have.
Remind me that they are my friends, not enemies,
that they are my teachers, not my wardens.

May I befriend the unwanted parts of myself
and continually learn wisdom from them.

Thank you for lovingly embracing me as I am while the murky layers of my many shortcomings are slowly transformed into love.

> *"She delivered . . . from transgression. . . . She protected (them) from (their) enemies, and kept (them) safe from those who lay in wait for (them)."*
> *Wisdom 10:1,12*

Journaling

Dialogue with one of your personal qualities that you would rather not have.

Ask Sophia how this quality has been, or can be, your teacher.

Friendship

Faithful Friend,
today I am immensely grateful for friends
who come in all shapes and flavors,
who love me as I am with my strengths
and with my never-may-be-transformed foibles.
I am keenly aware of their touches of goodness.
Their warm, considerate elements of care
are comfort and encouragement to me.
They leave my heart more open and alive.
I thank you for every friend I have,
for each one brings me a unique gift of love.

You, Cherished Wisdom, are astir amid all these loves.
You are the gold within every loving relationship.
You are the faithfulness in long-enduring friendships.
You are the energy of endless goodness in each of us.

Thank you for those who have let me into their hearts.
May I be a woman of love for all whom I meet.
May understanding and kindness be the gifts I give.
Today I hold in my heart those whom I call "friend,"

and I entrust them into your compassionate care.

I also bring with me the many in my world
who question if they are capable of being lovable,
those whose love has died, choked in the weeds
of bitterness, betrayal, doubt, or despair.
Keep reassuring those who feel friendless
that they have the ability to love and be loved.

> ". . . in kinship with Wisdom there is immortal-
> ity, and in friendship with her, pure delight."
> Wisdom 8:17

Journaling

Describe what you consider to be the key qualities
of a good friend.

Are any of these qualities similar to those you most
appreciate and admire in Holy Wisdom?

What helps you to be a good friend? What keeps you
from being a good friend?

Write a letter of gratitude to a good friend of yours.

Generativity

Generous Giver of Life,
as I look at autumned Earth today,
I marvel at her gracious generosity,
at her willingness to share her gifts.
The harvesting has begun,
and fields full of ripened grain
are stripped of their abundance.
A summer full of intense growing
is swept away by huge, hungry machines.
As I look at Earth's barrenness
after the reaping and gathering,
it seems to me she does not begrudge
the giving of that which grows and ripens.

Unlike Earth, I am not so gracious.
I want the fullness and the fruitfulness,
but I fight the emptiness of giving away.
May I have her grand spirit of generosity
and be willing to give of my own produce
for the future well-being of the cosmos.

Abundant Provider,
what is asked of me?
What is required?
What am I to give to this world,
I, who have received so much?

> *"She fills their whole house with desirable*
> *goods, and their storehouses with her produce."*
> *Ecclesiasticus 1:17*

Journaling

Draw a garden filled with an abundant harvest.

Let the fruits, vegetables, herbs, and flowers sym-
bolize the gifts (relationships, talents, experiences,
etc.) that are part of your life's produce.

Write a prayer about your garden of abundance.

Good-bye to Summer

Bestower of Fruitfulness,
little pockets of gold
sing among the green,
humming the melody
of autumn's arrival.
The calendar speaks
of no such thing,
but trees rarely lie.

Summer's vibrant swelling
of sweet fruitfulness
still entices me.
Cool mornings and ripe afternoons
are too delicious for me
to simply say "good-bye."

I grieve again summer's going.
I struggle once more to welcome
the dying inherent in autumn.

I turn to my heart,
where you dwell in harmony.

Together we will prepare
for this never-easy call
to say farewell to fruitfulness.

Wise Lady of the Seasons,
you sing a spiraling melody,
urging me onward with your song,
the only words of which I hear
are "let go, let go, let go."

> *"She is more precious than jewels*
> *and nothing you desire can compare with her."*
> *Proverbs 3:15*

Journaling

Is there a part of your life that is in "summer" now?

Are you being asked to let go of anything that has
been fruitful and abundant for you?

What part of your "summer" is most challenging for
you to let go?

Grief and Loss

Companion of the Sorrowing,
bind your love
strongly, fiercely,
to the memories
of my loved one
that are stored within me.
May they never wear out
when death grows distant.
I want to forever honor
and cherish the goodness
of my loved one's life.

Guardian of the Grieving,
lift up my sad heart.
Let me find laughter
in the midst of my loss.
Let me find hope
in the midst of my sadness.
Let me find comfort
in the midst of my emptiness.
Let me find meaning

in the midst of my confusion.
Let me find you,
ever-vigilant Beloved,
as my shelter and my solace.
Sustain my aching heart.

> *"Therefore I determined to take her to live with me, knowing that she would give me good counsel and encouragement in cares and grief."*
> *Wisdom 8:9*

Journaling

Recall a treasured memory of a loved one. Sip on it mentally and emotionally, like a glass of good red wine.

Write the memory down. Place it under your pillow or in your pocket.

Touch it often with tenderness.

Guidance

Trusted Guide,
you are my Mentor, my Inspiration,
my Home of good choices and decisions.
You help me to search with confidence
as I find my way to inner peace.

Please gather your wisdom around me.
Guide me carefully as I make choices
about how to use my energy positively.
Place your discerning touch on my mind
so that I will think clearly.
Place your loving fingers on my heart
so I will be more fully attentive
to what is really of value.

Teach me how to hear your voice,
to be aware of what is in my mind and heart,
to attend to your wisdom in those around me,
to acknowledge my intuitions and ponder my dreams,
to listen to the earth and all of life,
for in each piece of my existence you are guiding me.

Guide of my life,
thank you for all you have given to me.
Reveal my spiritual path
and direct me in the living of it.
Lead me to inner peace and oneness with you.

> *"She will guide me wisely in my actions."*
> *Wisdom 9:11*

Journaling

Search your present life situation. Where is it that you most need Sophia's guidance?

Go to Sophia. Find her sitting in her chair of wisdom. Ask her to lead and direct you.

Receive her wisdom.

Hope

Delight of my Heart,
I grow ever more grateful
as I pause to look over my shoulder,
reflecting on days gone by,
seeing how your counsel never leaves me.

Perhaps it is the terribly clean dawn
sweeping over the January land
that gifts my heart with a strong sense
of hope, of promise, of blessing.
Somewhere far down inside
I feel cherished and welcomed by you.
I believe you are drawing me ever closer,
with the whisper of "come" in the air.

Eternal Presence, all afire in me,
you breathe upon my embers, they glow.
Your ever-reaching love holds me
as I learn again to not be afraid.

Just as the light has given me morning,
so you, Holy One, have given me hope.

Praise to you for drawing me forward,
encouraging me to bid farewell to the past.

Continue to blow on the embers.
Light the fire again and again.
Flame it bright and full.
Gift me with surrender in love
so that I can be more fully yours.

> *"Wisdom rescued from troubles those who
> served her."*
> *Wisdom 10:9*

Journaling

Where do you find hope in your life?

Is there any area of your life that seems hopeless
and needs to be rekindled into a burning flame?

Inner Freedom

Liberating Spirit,
part of me has forgotten
the freedom of self-acceptance,
the putting aside of what others think,
the quieting of the inner voices
that demand, nag, and whine.

Part of me has stopped believing
in my potential for growth,
in the possibilities of my dreams,
in the grace of my prayer.

Part of me holds too tightly
to what the ego knows,
to securities that have grown stale,
to fears that stand in domination.

I want to remember
my inner wings.
I want to soar free
under the welcoming sky
of personal freedom.

Winged One, Free One,
enter my imprisoned self.
Break the bonds
that clasp my spirit.
Whisper in my soul's ear:
"Wings, wings,
remember your wings!"

> *"For wisdom is more mobile than any*
> *motion . . ."*
> *Wisdom 7:24*

Journaling

What would your life look like if you were more liberated and free?

What keeps you from remembering your wings?

Inner Garden

Gracious Gardener,
how wondrously you care for my soil.
You send your waters of refreshment.
You fertilize me with your wisdom.
You warm me with your enduring kindness.
You keep drawing me toward your light.

New growth continually sprouts
from the soil of my spiritual garden.
Flowers of creativity bloom.
Herbs of joy flavor my days.
Vegetables of nourishment flourish.

You constantly care for my garden,
weeding it when weaknesses grow tall,
turning the soil when the ground is hard,
comforting and protecting me
when enemies chew on my leaves.

Gracious Gardener,
I trust that you will continually
water my growing garden

and drench my flower beds
with your abiding love.

> *"I said, 'I will water my garden and drench*
> *my flower beds.'"*
> *Ecclesiasticus 24:31*

Journaling

Go with the Divine Gardener and take a look at your
spiritual garden.

How is it being tended?

What is flourishing there?

What kind of weeds are growing?

Does any of it need nourishment or fertilizing?

Is any of it dry and longing for a good watering?

Light-Bearer

Eternal Lamp of Love,
remind me often of how much radiance comes
from the glow of one small candle flame.
When my spiritual window is heavily clouded,
and your abiding love seems far from me,
restore my belief in your vibrant presence.
When I doubt my ability to be a bearer of your light,
shine your truth and wisdom into my faltering spirit.

Radiant Star in my heart,
in every generation you pass into holy souls.
Thank you for the illuminated beings
who have touched my life with their goodness.
Your light shining through them
has inspired me and filled me with spiritual energy.

Assure me that I can also be a Light-bearer for others,
a clear window of your eternal starlight.
Stir and whirl your dynamic presence in my being.
Stream your loving kindness through me.
I will open my mind and heart to your presence

as you greet me in the unexpected
and the challenging.
I, too, can make a difference in my world
because of your radiant light shining through me.
I am ready to pay the price for transparency.
May my desire for deeper union with you be realized.

> *"Her radiance never ceases . . . In every genera-
> tion she passes into holy souls."*
> *Wisdom 7:10,27*

Journaling

What part of you easily shines forth?

What part of you remains hidden?

Who are some of the people in your life who have
been Light-bearers for you?

Lighten Up

Holy Wisdom,
"lighten up," your graced voice urges,
as I dig my way deeper
into the paralysis of anxiety.

Immersed in my intensity,
bludgeoned with responsibility,
I focus on the thousand items
shouting at me from their precarious perch
while I wheeze with self-pity.

"Lighten up,"
your graced voice suggests
as I struggle in the net
of my desolate self-destruction.

Inundated with details and duties,
each clamoring for a morsel of my time,
my life is overpopulated with expectations
while my true loves are ignored and unfed.

When did I develop the notion
that I could do it all?

When did I smugly decide I could handle everything
without you by my side?

Slowly I become more grateful
for your strong, persistent voice
nudging me toward the laughter of letting go
and the chuckle of neglect.

> *"One who is vigilant on her account will soon*
> *be free from care."*
> *Wisdom 6:15*

Journaling

Is there any aspect of your life where you need to
"lighten up"?

What part does laughter and humor have in your
spiritual journey?

What keeps you stuck in busyness?

Listening to My Soul

Guardian of my Deepest Self,
I need to be still, to listen,
not only to falling leaves
and the gentle wind;
I need to listen to my soul,
too long neglected
while I bowed to the wild cries
of my greedy culture,
ever ravenous
for my undivided attention:
Do more, Buy more,
See more, Be more, Go more.

I am weary
with feeding this huge mouth
that devours my soul.

Let me be still
amid the beauty of earth.
Let me be a silent admirer
of all that is sacred.

Let me be reverent
in the presence of another.
Let me restore my inner eye.
Let me put to rest the wildness
of endless activity.

Let me end my seeking
the glitter of streets
that go nowhere.

> *"Hear, for I will speak noble things . . . for my*
> *mouth will utter truth."*
> *Proverbs 8:6*

Journaling

Who or what tries to devour your soul?

Who or what keeps you from giving your deepest
self your undivided attention?

What do you hear when you listen to your soul?

Live Each Day
with Awareness

Eternal Dwelling Place,
I know all things are passing.
My final home is not here.
Yet I zoom mindlessly through my days
missing the passionate gift of life.

How differently I would enter each day
if I embraced the shortness of my life span.
The things I consider inconveniences
would have a different colored hue.
The work I feel driven to accomplish
would pale beside relationships I cherish.
The irritations and the angers would dissolve
as I inhaled the preciousness of life.

Joyful Journeyer,
I hear you call to me this day:
"Behold! Enjoy! Appreciate!
Welcome all who enter this new day.
Live wild with rapturous wonder.

Look with awe and smile with elation.
Forgive those who stand at a distance.
Thank those who have settled in your heart.
Be tender with the rough edges of yourself.
Taste each morsel of life with fullness."

May I live each day with heartiness,
keeping things in clear perspective,
recognizing that this day before me might truly be
my last.

> *"For she is a breath of the power of God . . ."*
> *Wisdom 7:25*

Journaling

How would you live today if you knew it was your
last?

Whom would you thank?

Whom would you forgive or ask forgiveness?

What would you say to those who are significant in
your life?

Longing for a Spiritual Embrace

I am lonely for you, Beloved One,
I long for a sense of your embrace.
I know that contented feelings
have little to do with effective prayer,
but I still want assurance of your nearness.

My spiritual practices falter.
They fall apart like tiny pieces of plaster
on the floor of my dull and lifeless heart.
I fear my meditation each day
is an isolated, mental mumbling,
a cacophony of endless thoughts.

I turn to you with my plea:
free me from judging my prayer;
awaken my trust of your love;
instill me with peaceful acceptance.
Assure me of the exquisite value
of continued faithfulness to you.

I give you my passionate attention
as I listen to the seeming silence of your voice.

> *"Those who eat of me will hunger for more,*
> *and those who drink of me will thirst for more."*
> *Ecclesiasticus 24:21*

Journaling

What is your heart's deepest desire?

What do you hope to have happen in order to realize
this desire?

Express this longing in a song, a prayer, a psalm, or
some other form that resonates with you.

Lost in the Fog

Quiet Mystery,
today the earth wears mufflers on her ears.
Heavy wet clouds disguise the silent land.
The city is a giant mound of bleary white
with dense fog permeating everything.
Even the sparrow's song sounds thick.
In the concealing mist of morning,
street lights blur with masked revelation,
and walkers are lost in a veil of obscurity.

Secret One of my Soul,
portions of the land within me are dimly lit,
answers to my daily struggles are hazy,
and direction for my future lies hidden.
Often I lose my way as I meander in this inner fog,
struggling to find the path of some deeper peace.

As I reach out in this dim state of my inner domain,
I cry out for you and find you there,
safely leading me amid the mystery.
Quiet me, as fog quiets the external world,

so that I can listen more intently to you.
Draw me further into surrender.
Rest me in your comforting stillness,
and let me be content with what is unclear.

> *"I came forth from the mouth of the Most
> High, and covered the earth like a mist."*
> *Ecclesiasticus 24:3*

Journaling

What are the "foggy" areas in your life?

What aspects need greater clarity and vision?

How are you responding to these foggy areas?

Moving Beyond
Self-Centeredness

All-Embracing, Compassionate Companion,
You know me through and through.
You love me completely as I am.
You also know what challenges me,
how I need to continue to grow,
to constantly be more transformed.

Some of the loving pieces of my heart
stray away or hug themselves tightly
in the suffocating web of self-centeredness.
I get so caught up in "me" and "mine"
that I ignore those who are around me.
I sink so deeply into the mud of my own misery
that I neglect others who have great pain.
I feel so fully with the beauty of life
that I forget to share it with others.
I become so absorbed in my endless activity
that I focus only on satisfying myself.

In doing this, I miss constant opportunities
to be a person whose reach is far and deep.

Perceptive One,
teach me how to be attentive to my own well-being,
and to also recognize and respond to others in need.
Be the great balancer of my inner world.
Be the eyes and ears of my heart.
Do not let me wrap myself entirely around "me."
Draw me out from my inward gaze.
Join my heart to the expansiveness of your love.
Take me to all who await my compassionate attention.

> *"Lay aside immaturity, and live,*
> *and walk in the way of insight."*
> *Proverbs 9:6*

Journaling

In one column, write "Me," in another write
"Others." List words/phrases under each one that
name your concerns and your activities.

Look at your two lists. What do they tell you about
your approach to life? Is there anything you need or
want to change or re-balance?

Nature Revitalizes
My Soul

Womb of Wonder,
all of creation has your life-giving touch.
When I come and bow humbly before you,
I see how your wisdom breathes in everything.
In these sacred seeing moments
I learn and relearn truths that free me.

I discover endurance from a weathered stone.
I recognize my illusions in the changing skies.
I know your ceaseless tune in a whippoorwill's call.
I hear your heartbeat in the lapping of lake water.
I find release of sorrow in the tears of gentle rain.
I recover my lost humor watching young foxes at play.
I see your protective love
revealed through a mother duck.

When I enter into the domain of your creation,
things begin to settle, to become quiet in me,
like a windy harbor calming with the sunset.
It is there that I find the needed reassurance

to stay in the struggle and challenge of life.
It is then that I find restored clarity
about the "why and wherefore" of how things are.

O Breath of Creation,
lead me often to your realm of nature
where you revivify the lost energy of my spirit.

> *"(The Creator) poured her out . . . upon all the
> living . . ."*
> *Ecclesiasticus 1:9*

Journaling

Find a place where you can sit quietly with something from nature (a plant, a tree, clouds, a stone,
birds . . .)

Just "be" with this part of creation for a while and let
it speak to you.

What do you hear?

Non-judgment

Unconditional Lover, the days fly by.
I run to catch my breath.
Underneath my hurry and rush
smug judges try to take over.
They speak with resentment,
chiding voices of envy and scorn.
They rule harshly against others,
unleash their poisonous tongues,
and pronounce their deadly decisions
with unkind, critical judgments.

Great Heart of Love,
help me to look with soft eyes
upon all who are a part of my days.
Break through the barriers
of my scrutinizing views.
Transform my inner landscape
into a peaceful place of acceptance.
Pull back my projections and criticisms.
Replace my mean measurements
and my biased expectations

with an openness that allows others to be,
without conformity to my censure.

Restore the simple acceptance
that was in my heart
when I was newly birthed.
Cleanse me of the cultural standards
that soil my perceptions
and keep me from being kind.

> *"Send her forth . . . that I may learn what is*
> *pleasing to you."*
> *Wisdom 9:11*

Journaling

How is your inner landscape? Any "smug judges"
there?

What is the quality of the observation and awareness
that you have of others?

Invite Sophia to visit your inner landscape as you
consider its condition.

Openness

Surprising One,
snow in September
stretches me into December,
tugs at my fixed notions
of how seasons happen,
unravels my theories
of how things should be.

When I allow myself to be open,
I see beauty everywhere,
dancing like your divine spirit
in the birthing of creation.
I can view your surprises
with clear eyes,
uncluttered with expectations
of how things ought to look.

When I am closed,
my well-guarded views cling
like grandfather barnacles,

hindering my ability
to be amazed or surprised.

Beauty-Giver,
in every piece of my life
you wait to astonish me.
You call to me,
with the voice of urgency,
"Be open to life, be open,
lest you miss the treasures
awaiting you in the unexpected."

> *"She hastens to make herself known
> to those who desire her."*
> Wisdom 6:13

Journaling

Recall a situation in which you struggled to be open,
in which you eventually found treasures in the
unexpected. What did you discover?

What is currently your greatest hindrance to being
open?

Let Sophia, the Beauty-Giver, open your mind and
heart. What do you see?

Patience

Juicy Life-Giver,
over and over you teach me
about the process of inner growth:
first the green shoot,
then the bud,
finally the flowering.

No instant-zap blooming
on the spiritual path,
no pressured pursuit of growth,
no room for controlled management.

You look at me with your springtime eyes
and whisper to my impatient heart:
"Lean back, relax, be receptive
while you wait, wait, wait,
for the transforming juices to flow."

You keep advising me
to put the brakes on my desire
for a fast transformation,

74

to slow down the revving engines
of my impatient anticipation.

You encourage me
to rest in your arms of trust,
to wait for my slow blooming,
for it will come with the sureness
of your ever-evolving grace
and the wisdom
of your ever-enduring love.

> *"Come to her like one who plows and sows, and
> wait for her good harvest."*
> *Ecclesiasticus 6:19*

Journaling

What is most difficult for you to wait for in your
spiritual growth?

How is your patience?

As you wait, what do you need from Sophia?

Peeling Off
Another Layer

Transforming Presence,
layers and layers of my false self
keep being stripped away from me.
I walk with caterpillar feet,
knowing that the skin must be shed
time and again
before I find my butterfly wings.

I look at the old discarded peelings
of the person I thought I was
with some dismay and sadness,
but also with some relief and joy.

With every lifted layer, I feel lighter.
With every painful peeling, I am freer.
With every discarded skin, I stretch deeper.
With every sloughed off segment, I grow wiser.

Keep teaching me, Freedom Bringer,
that it is never too late

to embrace the changes
that lead to my truest self.
Keep nudging me away from confining security
when I cling too tightly to what needs to go.

Continue to attune my spirit to your song
of ongoing transformation.
Remind me daily that I will always have another
layer that needs to be shed.

> *"There is in her a spirit that, is . . . unique,*
> *manifold, subtle, . . . clear . . . unpolluted . . ."*
> *Wisdom 7:22*

Journaling

Take a look at the last layer that peeled off of "you."

What did you find beneath that layer?

What did you have to leave behind?

How has this made a difference in your life?

Releasing Feelings

Comforting Mother,
take me in your arms and hold me close.
Give me room to shed my tears.
Grant me strength to meet my anger.
Help me to release the dormant, painful emotions
that keep me from peace and contentment.

I lean on your bosom and find solace there.
The strong pull of your nurturing love
gives me the courage to not run away.
I can meet the feelings that haunt my dreams.
I can face the emotions that crave my attention.

Let me slowly find and embrace the leftover grief,
the unwept tears, the unattended pain.
They are buried in years of keeping busy,
lost in the accumulation of neglect,
hidden in a heart so heavy with hurt
that the voice of the past could not be heard.

Support, comfort, and tenderly nurture me
as I befriend these voices of pain.

Enfold me in your healing embrace
while I bid farewell to these ancient sores.

> *"She will come . . . like a mother . . . (they) will*
> *lean on her and not fall."*
> *Ecclesiasticus 15:2*

Journaling

Let Sophia, the Great Mother, gather you in her arms.

Receive her comfort.

Tell her of any leftover pain that still dwells within you.

Sabbath Time

Queen of the Quiet Places,
thank you for Sunday mornings
flavored with Sabbath stillness.
The only sounds
breaking the immense quiet
are crickets humming
and the first yawns
of robins and cardinals.

The half moon waxing
takes to her pillow
while the sun dances,
spreading out wings of dawn,
edged in pink and gold.

Even the oak leaves
are quietly attentive
while the wind waits
to stir the day into motion.

My soul awakens with ease,
cradled in meditation,

sung to by your stillness,
Silent Sentinel of my Soul.

And I am delivered
for a while
from the torture
of endless schedules
and the deafening noise of my own desires.

> *"When I enter my house, I shall find rest with her."*
> *Wisdom 8:16*

Journaling

Where do you find Sabbath time?

What brings you the greatest of stillness and ease of mind and heart?

Singer in My Soul

Singer in my Soul!
I long for your song
in my empty heart.
Is there a place
where you can hang
your notes?
If not, whisper them,
in the thin air.

Chant little threads
of your wisdom
in the hollow spaces
of my emptiness.

Sing me the old stories
that strengthen me,
stories of your beauty,
tales of your compassion.

Enter into my day
with the tender press
of your unfailing love.

Singer in my Soul,
arouse my listless spirit
with the sweet sound
of your hidden presence,
and the gracious melody
of your continual kindness.

> *"There is a spirit in her that is . . . irresistible,*
> *Beneficent, humane, steadfast, sure."*
> *Wisdom 7:22*

Journaling

What kind of song is Sophia singing in your soul today?

You may want to hum a melody that resonates with this song in you.

Solitude

Companion of my Solitude,
sometimes I think that half of me
is well-lodged in another world.
On rainy days, in times of solitude,
my spirit pulls and tugs,
crying for home in that other space.
All the things here
that give my life rhyme and reason
fade from view.
I am left with the longing
to put down my sword
of busyness
and dwell in the land
of simple contemplation.

Raindrops on the cottage roof,
bird songs in the woods,
the taste of morning air,
the stillness of the woods,
all these draw me beyond
to where the other half dwells.

Companion of my Solitude,
keep encouraging me to take time
for my inward journey.
Help me to be faithful
to this essential element of my life.

"Come to me, you who desire me . . ."
Ecclesiasticus 10:19

Journaling

What do you appreciate most about solitude?

What do you least appreciate about it?

What is your life like when you do not have any solitude in it?

Spiritual Richness

Sophia, Feast-Giver,
you have set a table before me
replete with spiritual richness,
laden with all I need for my growth,

How boundlessly you bless,
how generously you give,
how completely you love,
how faithfully you provide,
how tenderly you understand,
how fully you forgive,
how endlessly you invite,
how willingly you welcome,
how lovingly you cherish,
how compassionately you shelter.

The riches of your presence
exceed my largest dreams.
The fullness of your kindness
expands beyond my expectations.

Unreservedly you display your riches.
You freely offer all of them to me,
a banquet of daily nourishment,
plentiful food to fill my hungry soul.
I have only to come to the table
to receive from your abundant feast.

> *"Come, eat of my bread and drink of the wine*
> *I have mixed. . . . Come to me, you who desire*
> *me, and eat your fill of my fruits."*
> *Proverbs 9:5; Ecclesiasticus 24:19*

Journaling

What does the table of Sophia's feast offer to you?

Which "foods" do you partake of easily?

Which "foods" do you avoid?

Draw a table of Sophia's feast with the spiritual richness you have known.

Springtime Prayer

O Dancer of Creation,
the earth awakens to an urgent call to grow.
In the hidden recesses of my wintered spirit
I, too, hear the humming of your voice,
calling me, wooing my deadness back to life.

My soul yawns, stretches, quickens,
as the energy of Spring revives my weariness.
I sit with wonder, observing the steady activity
of downy woodpeckers and newly yellowed finch.
I do so with the avid attention of a child's first look,
savoring the colors and shapes of earth's loveliness.

As the filtering patterns of early sunlight
lift the shades of green in every growing thing,
I enter into spring's unlettered words of life.
For a while my doubts, anxieties, and worries
become like chapters in some ancient book
whose text no longer claims my full attention.
I am content to sit, watching Spring
turn the pages of this animated publication,

eager to discover the invigorating story
reflected in my own springtime revelation.

Tell me, Wise Awakener,
why is it easier to believe in a stem of new grass,
or the opening bud of a fresh purple crocus,
than it is to believe in the greening of me?

> *"If riches are a desirable possession in life,*
> *what is richer than wisdom, the active cause*
> *of all things?"*
> *Wisdom 8:5*

Journaling

What is Sophia awakening within you?

What seeks to be revived?

Find a seed. Hold it in your hand. Let it tell you
about something in you that needs to be urged back
to life.

Stream of Enduring Love

Stream of Enduring Love,
I yearn to have a feeling of oneness with you.
I wish I felt a driving passion, an insatiable thirst.
Instead, there's just this steady hum of fidelity,
with an occasional flicker of intense longing.

Each day I deliberately place myself
in the midst of your stream of enduring love.
I want so much to feel spiritual refreshment,
to have your divine passion sweep over me
with the power of an energizing waterfall.

Stream of Enduring Love,
I must let go of my desire to desire.
You provide for what I need.
You keep my heart alive in your love.
More than this I do not need,
but my ego clamors greedily for more.

I will rest in the stream of your goodness,
let your enduring love quietly wash over me,
be grateful for all that I have.

I will quiet that incessant voice in me
that whines for something more.

> *"All good things came to me along with
> her . . ."*
> *Wisdom 7:11*

Journaling

Have you ever whined or gotten impatient in your
desire for a more deeply felt sense of Sophia's love?

Have you ever experienced "spiritual greed"?

Write about your experience of or longing for
Sophia's enduring love.

Sunrise Prayer

Maker of the Morning,
as the blazing sun glories the eastern horizon,
I arise and greet this new day.
My spirit bows with gratitude,
rejoicing in hope for what this day promises.

Focusing Ray of Light,
I celebrate the fresh, penetrating clarity
of your daily entrance into my life,
stronger than the rising sun of morning,
clearer than brilliant light on a maple leaf.

As people of the sleepy earth stretch and stir,
awaken in them an eagerness for your wisdom.
As creatures come forth from their hidden places,
protect them from human greed and carelessness.
May this day be a day of peace for all of creation,
with your touch of compassion extended to each one.

I commit all that awakens in my heart
into the gracious hands of your care.
I dedicate all I am and all I do this day to you,

the Radiant One of the morning.
I entrust my entire being into the protective arms
   of your love

Creator of the Dawning Sun,
draw me with your eternal energy.
Filter your transforming glow
through every inner fiber of mine
until I am transparent
with the power of your enlightening beauty.

> *"Whoever loves her loves life, and those who*
> *seek her from early morning are filled with joy."*
> *Ecclesiasticus 4:12*

Journaling

What is the intention of your heart as you arise?

Consider how you might want to start your day with Sophia.

Compose a greeting to the Maker of Morning that is reflective of your hopes, dreams, and desires for the day.

Taking Risks

Divine Challenger,
when did I stop risking?
When did I lose my edge
for adventure and surprise?
When did I start pretending
that what I now know
is all there is to know?
When did I give in to fear
and bow to security?

When did I let uncertainty
press against my free spirit?
When did I start moving
toward the easy, sure thing?
When did I give away
my ability to be disturbed?
When did I start refusing to
pay the price
for fuller depth and joy?
When did I let panic
of the unknown future

wrap its barbed wire fingers
around my desire to grow?

Inner Source of Courage,
nudge me toward my growth.
Urge me away from my strongholds.
Convince me of my potential
to leap beyond the barriers.

> *"And if anyone longs for wide experience, she
> knows the things of old, and infers the things
> to come."*
> *Wisdom 8:8*

Journaling

What are the challenges in your life?

Who and what encourages you to take risks?

Who and what holds you back?

How willing are you to let go of security in order to
grow?

The Dry Creek-bed

Dear Sophia,
thank you for helping me to see
how my inner life is like that little creek
at the bottom of the hill.
Only a few times during the year
is it a genuine rushing stream,
filled to overflowing.
Mostly it just slowly trickles,
steady, quiet, and unobtrusive.

There are long, parched months
when the creek-bed is almost totally dry,
with the merest wet thread
announcing its unhurried movement.
But always the creek-bed is there,
an open, uncluttered space, ready
to receive rains that eventually come.

I, too, am a dry creek-bed,
with a trickle of life moving silently along.
I, too, need a steadfast space,

ready and receptive,
to welcome your abundance.

Teach me the value of waiting
for insight, consolation, and joy.
Turn me toward greater trust.
Help me to believe more fully
that what I need will come flowing
into the dry creek-bed of my life.

> *"For at last you will find the rest she gives;*
> *and she will be changed into joy for you."*
> *Ecclesiasticus 6:28*

Journaling

When has your creek-bed been the driest?

When has your creek-bed been filled to
overflowing?

What is the condition of your creek-bed now?

The Heart of a Child

Dear Lover of Life,
last night as neighborhood children
were delightfully at play,
memories of my childhood on the farm stirred in me.
I remembered playing contentedly in the grove,
where I would have to be called in after dark.
I lived so much in the present moment then.
Now I almost always have one foot in the future,
missing a lot of the pleasure and beauty of the "now."

I have forgotten what it is like to be fully alive.
I have become a functional, productive, serious adult.
What grasps my enthusiasm, my love of life,
and drags it down to the cellar and locks it up?
What causes me to neglect my deepest needs?
What leads me to be overly-giving and responsible?
How can I let your creative, invigorating presence
be more fully alive and active in my life?

Leaping Voice of Freedom,
help me to reclaim my Inner Child.

Keep calling to me:
"Enter wholeheartedly into an embrace of life.
Do not be afraid of what others think.
Let go of your fears for economic security,
Hang loose with your need to 'get it all done.'
You were meant to enjoy this life I have given you.
Come to me. I will set you free."

> *"I was daily (the Creator's) delight . . . rejoicing
> in (the) inhabited world and delighting in the
> human race."*
> *Proverbs 8:30-31*

Journaling

Draw or paint a picture of your Inner Child.

Give this Child a name.

Write a dialogue with your Inner Child about your experience of life as you now know it. (Be sure to use your less-dominant writing hand when your Inner Child is speaking.)

Time to Surrender

Source of Strength,
as I drove in the late afternoon sunlight
radiant with golden beams, you graced me again.
I became aware of how I must surrender to you,
trust you with the cares and worries I bear.
I need to rely on you, count on your strength,
open my hands, and give all my concerns to you,
placing them under the shelter of your wings.
You are waiting to be my refuge and my comfort,
if only I will turn to you and receive your care.

I see again how I become too independent
when I am straining with the toughness of life.
I try to go it alone, do it all myself.
How quickly I forget your compassionate presence
as I push to have my way, no matter what.

Help me to be more alert when I fall backward
into the pit of this old, controlling behavior.
Remind me that there is sufficient strength
when I allow myself to lean on you,

that there is much assurance and hope
when I remember to trust in your guidance.

Comfort me. Lead me through these difficult days.
May I feel your peace enfolding me with ease.
Bring me often to the center of my heart
where you dwell with ease and confidence.

> *"Put your feet into her fetters, and your neck*
> *into her collar. Bend your shoulders and carry*
> *her, and do not fret under her bonds. . . . Then*
> *her fetters will become for you a strong*
> *defense, and her collar a glorious robe."*
> *Ecclesiasticus 6:24-25, 29*

Journaling

What part of your heart needs to lean on your Inner
Source of Strength but finds it difficult to do?

What keeps you from surrendering to Sophia?

Transformation

Source of Transformation,
my heart begs your entrance
even as it fights and holds you off.
One hand of mine reaches out to you,
but the other hides behind my back,
shunning your will and your way for me.
Your coming is not always gentle;
sometimes it sears with painful truth.
While I cry out for you to come,
another part of me whispers,
"But not so near as to change me."

When will I freely embrace you?
When will I let go of my old ways?
When will I be vulnerable?
When will I acknowledge my need of you?
When will I learn to give you my all?

Enter and rest in my shadows
until they finally give up their dark.
Come, fill my being with your love,

until your transforming radiance
is the only lasting thing.

> *"Although she is but one, she can do all things,*
> *and while remaining in herself she renews all*
> *things."*
> *Wisdom 7:27*

Journaling

What attitude or behavior of yours cries out to be
transformed?

Draw a symbol of this attitude or behavior, or write
a memo to yourself about this.

Keep it in a place where it will often remind you of
your need to be transformed.

Winter

Source of Courage for my Soul,
your season of winter teaches me
about the dark season inside of me.
All the old external props fall away in winter,
nothing to rely on except the whisper of faith.

In the light of a summer's brilliant day,
it is easy to be brave and confident,
but inside of winter, I stumble blindly,
seeking what I so easily fed on in the light.
This winter journey demands steel courage,
firm determination, fierce boldness,
a heart unyielding to the phantoms of fear
and the menacing moans of despair.

When I stay on this inward road,
true abundance becomes known.
Winter shows what summer never could:
the core of what I believe and value,
the sum of who and what I love.
I learn the enormous power of endurance

and the gift of accepting and loving
who I truly am.

Wise Spirit of the Darkness,
take my hand and teach me to be unafraid
of the wild winds of my inner winter.
Lead me through the gloomy valleys
and teach me how to walk in the dark.

> *"She guided them along a marvelous way, and
> became a shelter to them by day, and a starry
> flame through the night."*
> *Wisdom 10:17*

Journaling

How has Sophia been your teacher and guide in
your inner winters?

What have you learned from Sophia about walking
in the dark?

Wordless Praise
to Sophia

Wise One who claims my heart,
how can I name you to others?
How can I ever capture
the reflection of your radiance
rising in profuse grandeur
on the glittering sea of my soul?
It is like trying to capture
the essence of a harvest moon
rising in full orange orbness,
sparkling glory on a September sea.

Some moments have no words.
Some relationships have no narration.
They rise silently like the swelling path
of the full moon in a harvest sky,
like the soundless rise and fall
on the breath of one who sleeps gently.

No need to capture, control, contain,
only to be present to the rising,

only to be aware of the silent breathing,
only to be with the unexpected illumination.

It is enough to rest in your love.
It is enough to taste your goodness.
It is enough to call you by name.
It is enough. It is enough.

> *"The first (one) did not know wisdom fully, nor*
> *will the last one fathom her."*
> *Ecclesiasticus 24:29*

Reflect upon a time when you felt a deep oneness
with Sophia, Holy Wisdom.

Recall the sweet essence of this sacred moment.
Taste the consolation and conviction of the love that
you felt. Sophia is with you now.

Write a psalm of love to her.

SOPHIA BIBLICAL PASSAGES

Proverbs
1:20–33
3:18
4:5–9
8:1–36
9:1–6

Ecclesiasticus
(also known as Sirach)
4:12–18
6:18–31
14:20–27
15:1–10
24:1–29
51:13–22

The Book of Wisdom
(also known as The Wisdom of
    Solomon)
6:12–17
7:7–14
7:22–30
8:1–18
9:9–11
10:1–21
11:1–26

Baruch
3:29–38
4:1–4

The book of Ecclesiastes (also known
as Qoheleth) is also a part of the wisdom literature in the Bible. However,
in this book wisdom is viewed as a
quality or thing. The twelve chapters
contain a collection of wisdom sayings and reflections about wisdom

given for guidance and understanding
in life.

Job is also included in the wisdom
literature because it, too, consists of
a study of human nature, God, and
the meaning of life. There are only a
few verses, however, that are directly
related to Sophia: Job 28:20–23.

There are others who would include
several of the psalms, some of the
sayings of Jesus, etc. as wisdom literature, but the above named books
of the Bible are those accepted by
most scholars as the "biblical wisdom
literature."

THEME INDEX

Theme Index

BIBLIOGRAPHY

Aldredge-Clanton, Jann. *In Search of the Christ-Sophia: An Inclusive Christology for Liberating Christians*. Mystic, CT: Twenty Third Publications, 1995.

Baring, Anne, and Andrew Harvey. *The Divine Feminine: Exploring the Feminine Face of God Around the World*. Berkeley, CA: Conari Press, 1996.

Bergant, Dianne. *What Are They Saying About Wisdom Literature?* Mahwah, NJ: Paulist Press, 1984.

Carr, Anne E. *A Search For Wisdom: Thomas Merton's Theology of the Self*. Notre Dame, IN: University of Notre Dame Press, 1990.

Cole, Susan, Marian Ronan, and Hal Taussig. *Wisdom's Feast: Sophia in Study and Celebration*. Kansas City, MO: Sheed and Ward, 1997.

Cunneen, Sally. *In Search of Mary: The Woman and the Symbol*. New York: Ballantine Books, 1996.

Daughters of Wisdom: Who is Wisdom-Sophia? (Meditations Based on "Love of Eternal Wisdom" by St. Louis deMontfort.) Litchfield, CT: Wisdom House.

Eisler, Rianne. *The Chalice and the Blade*. San Francisco: Harper San Francisco, 1988.

Fiorenza, Elizabeth Schüssler. *In Memory of Her*. New York: Crossroad, 1984. (c.f. pp. 130–140, "The Sophia-God of Jesus and the Discipleship of Women")

Fiorenza, Elisabeth Schüssler. *Sharing Her Word: Feminist Biblical Interpretation in Context*. Boston: Beacon Press, 1998.

Johnson, Elizabeth A. *She Who Is: The Mystery of God in Feminist Theological Discourse*. New York: Crossroad, 1993.

Matthews, Caitlin. *Sophia Goddess of Wisdom: The Divine Feminine, from Black Goddess to World Soul*. San Francisco: Harper San Francisco, 1993.

McFague, Sallie. *Metaphorical Theology: Models of God in Religious Language*. Philadelphia: Fortress Press, 1997.

Meehan, Mary Bridget. *Exploring the Feminine Face of God*. Kansas City, MO: Sheed and Ward, 1991.

Mollenkott, Virginia Ramey. *The Divine Feminine: The Biblical Imagery of God as Female*. New York: Crossroad, 1993.

O'Connor, Kathleen M. *The Wisdom Literature*. Wilmington, DE: Michael Glazier, 1988.

Powell, Robert A. *Divine Sophia, Holy Wisdom*. Nicasio, CA: The Sophia Foundation of North America, 1997.

Rupp, Joyce. *The Star In My Heart: Discovering Inner Wisdom*. Notre Dame, IN: Ave Maria Press, 2010.

Schipflinger, Thomas. *Sophia-Maria: A Holistic Vision of Creation*. York Beach, ME: Samuel Weiser, Inc., 1998.

Schneiders, Sandra. *Woman and the Word: The Gender of God in the New Testament and the Spirituality of Women*. Mahweh, NJ: Paulist Press, 1986.

Winter, Miriam Therese. *WomanWord: A Feminist Lectionary and Psalter on Women of the New Testament*. New York: Crossroad, 1990.

JOYCE RUPP is well known for her work as a writer, spiritual midwife, international retreat leader, and conference speaker. She is the author of numerous bestselling books, including *Praying Our Goodbyes*, *Open the Door*, *Fragments of Your Ancient Name*, and *Boundless Compassion*. *Fly While You Still Have Wings* earned an award in the spirituality books category from the Catholic Press Association. Rupp is a member of the Servite (Servants of Mary) community and the codirector of the Servite Center of Compassion's Boundless Compassion program. She lives in West Des Moines, Iowa.

Bibliography

AUDIO

Powell, A., Robert. *The Sophia Teachings: The Emergence of the Divine Feminine in Our Time.* (6 cassette tape set) Sounds True, Box 8010, Boulder, CO 80306.

MUSIC

Christian, Kathryn. *Ascension.* Notre Dame, IN: Ave Maria Press, 1999.

Fullmer, Colleen. *Dancing Sophia's Circle.* Loretto Spirituality Network: 725 Calhoun St., Albany, CA 94706. 1995.

Howard, Julie. *We Are the Circle: Celebrating the Feminine in Song and Ritual.* Collegeville, MN: The Liturgical Press, 1993.

Miriam Therese Winter and the Medical Mission Sisters. *Hymns Re-Imagined.* 77 Sherman St, Hartford, CT 06105, 860-233-0875, mms@hartsem.edu.

S O P H I A *Institutes/Organizations*

Sancta Sophia Seminary
22 Summit Ridge Dr.
Tahlequah, OK 74464
www.sanctasophia.org

Sophia Center
(A Wisdom School Celebrating Earth, Art & Spirit)
Holy Names College
3500 Mountain Blvd.
Oakland, CA 94619-1699
www.hnu.edu/sophia